MOUNTAIN SONGS

Selections from the Psalms with prayer meditations

PHOTOS BY:	PAGE:
Benny Alex:	42, 43, 46-47
Louis Bertrand:	3
Willi Burkhardt:	Cover, 6-7, 18-19, 20-21, 60-61, 62-63, 74—75
Siegfried Eigstler:	50-51, 52-53, 68-69
Bent Hansen:	16
Bildarchiv Huber:	4-5
Jørgen Vium Olesen:	12-13, 14, 17, 22-23, 26-27, 28-29, 32, 34-35, 38-39, 40-41, 48-49, 54-55, 56, 58-59, 66, 67, 70-71, 72-73
Otto Pfenninger:	76-77
Ulrik & Marco Schneiders:	78
Flemming Walsøe:	8-9, 10-11, 15, 24-25, 30, 31, 33, 44-45, 57, 64-65
Fred Wirz:	36-37

Printed in Hong Kong by South Sea International Press Ltd.,

ISBN 87 87732 56 4

MOUNTAIN SONGS

elections from the Psalms with prayer meditations

Edited by Jørgen Vium Olesen
Text by Marlee Alex
Scripture text from The Holy Bible, New International Version

Scandinavia

For who is God,
except the Lord? And
who is a rock, except
our God? It is God who arms
me with strength, And makes my way
perfect. He makes my feet
like the feet of deer,
And sets me on my
high places.

What is man that
You are mindful of
him, And the son of man that
You visit him? For You have made him
a little lower than the angels,
And You have crowned him
with glory and honor.

Happy Are Those

Whatever he does propers.

Blessed is the man who does not walk in the counsel of the wicked or stand in the way of sinners or sit in the seat of mockers.

But his delight is in the law of the Lord, and on his law he meditates day and night.

He is like a tree planted by streams of water, which yields its fruit in season and whose leaf does not wither. Whatever he does prospers.

Not so the wicked! They are like chaff that the wind blows away.

Therefore the wicked will not stand in the judgment, nor sinners in the assembly of the righteous.

For the Lord watches over the way of the righteous, but the way of the wicked will perish.

I've got my roots in the river. Those roots keep me from being where I should not be. The tumbling river waters are my daily miracle, not only keeping me alive, but growing. I've got my roots in the word of God, and I wouldn't change places with anybody anywhere.

The Lord Reigns

I have installed my King on Zion, my holy hill.

Why do the nations rage and the peoples plot in vain?
The kings of the earth take their stand and the rulers
gather together against the Lord and against his
Anointed One.
"Let us break their chains," they say, "and throw off
their fetters."
The One enthroned in heaven laughs; the Lord scoffs at
them.
Then he rebukes them in his anger and terrifies them in
his wrath, saying,
"I have installed my King on Zion, my holy hill."

*Some people assume that believing
in you, Lord, means I have to restrict
my possibilities and repress my joy.
These people choose to
misunderstand and misinterpret your
word. You merely laugh at them,
waiting for the appropriate moment to
astound them with the magnitude of
your purpose.*

Ask, and I Will Give You

Blessed are all who take refuge in him.

I will proclaim the decree of the Lord:
  He said to me, "You are my Son; today I have become your Father.
Ask of me, and I will make the nations your inheritance, the ends of the earth your possession.
You will rule them with an iron scepter; you will dash them to pieces like pottery."

Therefore, you kings, be wise; be warned, you rulers of the earth.
Serve the Lord with fear and rejoice with trembling.
Kiss the Son, lest he be angry and you be destroyed in your way, for his wrath can flare up in a moment.

The Good Shepherd has given his life for his sheep. Redemption is complete. All the horizons of the earth, every rocky mountain top, each grassy vale rejoices in this truth while the kings of the earth are silent, ignorent, ignoring. His sheep graze in safety for they have trusted him.

I Am Not Afraid

To the Lord I cry aloud, and he answers me from his holy hill.

O Lord, how many are my foes! How many rise up against me!
Many are saying of me, "God will not deliver him." — Selah
But you are a shield around me, O Lord, my Glorious One, who lifts up my head.
To the Lord I cry aloud, and he answers me from his holy hill. — Selah
I lie down and sleep; I wake again, because the Lord sustains me.
I will not fear the tens og thousands drawn up against me on every side.
Arise, O Lord! Deliver me, O my God! For you have struck all my enemies on the jaw; you have broken the teeth of the wicked.
From the Lord comes deliverance. May your blessing be on your people. — Selah.

Disappointment in other people is a universal experience. When we open ourselves to others we risk wounded spirits or bruised egos. When I am disappointed I rush into the presence of the Lord. His compassion envelopes me and makes me aware of more important realities.

He Hears Me

The Lord will hear when I call to him.

Answer me when I call to you, O my righteous God. Give me relief from my distress; be merciful to me and hear my prayer.

How long, O men, will you turn my glory into shame? How long will you love delusions and seek false gods? Know that the Lord has set apart the godly for himself; the Lord will hear when I call to him.

In your anger do not sin; when you are on your beds, search your hearts and be silent. — Selah

Offer right sacrifices and trust in the Lord.

Many are asking, "Who can show us any good?" Let the light of your face shine upon us, O Lord. You have filled my heart with greater joy than when their grain and new wine abound. I will lie down and sleep in peace, for you alone, O Lord, make me dwell in safety.

Time after time you patiently listened to my worried pleas. You answered each one after stretching my faith-muscles just a bit more. I knew that without it it is impossible to please you, but I did not believe I had enough faith until the crisis passed. Then I realized that even faith is given as a gift.

Voice in the Morning

You are not a God who takes pleasure in evil.

Give ear to my words, O Lord, consider my sighing.
Listgen to my cry for help, my King and my God, for to
you I pray.
Morning by morning, O Lord, you hear my voice;
morning by morning I lay my requests before you and
wait in expectation.

You are not a God who takes pleasure in evil; with you
the wicked cannot dwell.
The arrogant cannot stand in your presence; you hate all
who do wrong.
You destroy those who tell lies; bloodthirsty and
deceitful men the Lord abhors.

But I, by your great mercy, will come into your house;
in reverence will I bow down toward your holy temple.

Spring mornings I roam the tiny paths
in my garden searching for the first
green seedlings or brand new buds. I
feel close to you, look up to you, Lord.
For you love your garden too. You
delight in the tiniest sign of
newness, weeding out the useless,
promising a harvest ahead.

Sing for Joy

But let all who take refuge in you be glad.

Lead me, O Lord, in your righteousness because of my enemies — make straight your way before me.

Not a word from their mouth can be trusted; their heart is filled with destruction. Their throat is an open grave; with their tongue they speak deceit.

Declare them guilty, O God! Let their intrigues be their downfall. Banish them for their many sins, for they have rebelled against you.

But let all who take refuge in you be glad; let them ever sing for joy. Spread your protection over them, that those who love your name may rejoice in you.

For surely, O Lord, you bless the righteous; you surround them with your favor as with a shield.

Your name is my bank account, Lord. You encourage me to draw from it anytime. When I study its different expressions in the Bible I'm amazed at the wealth I possess. But I love your name for more than what it gives me. It is a pathway leading straight to your heart.

He shall be
like a tree
Planted by the
rivers of water,
That brings
forth its fruit
in its season,
Whose leaf
also shall
not wither;
And whatever
he does
shall prosper.

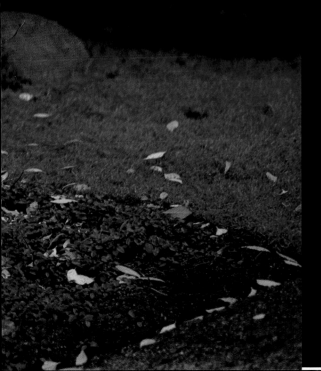

Rescue Me from Death

The Lord has heard my cry for mercy; the Lord accepts my prayer.

O Lord, do not rebuke me in your anger or discipline me in your wrath.
Be merciful to me, Lord, for I am faint; O Lord, heal me, for my bones are in agony.
My soul is in anguish. How long, O Lord, how long?

Turn, O Lord, and deliver me; save me because of your unfailing love.
No one remembers you when he is dead. Who praises you from the grave?

I am worn out from groaning; all night long I flood my bed with weeping and drench my couch with tears.
My eyes grow weak with sorrow; they fail because of all my foes.

Away from me, all you who do evil, for the Lord has heard my weeping.
The Lord has heard my cry for mercy; the Lord accepts my prayer.
May all my enemies be ashamed and dismayed; may they turn back in sudden disgrace.

*I've learned that when my child is
unruly it is usually an unconcious cry
for help. An inner wound may be
festering, a recent bruise still sore.
Eventually, the real problem
surfaces. You are far more sensitive
to me, Lord. Your interpret all signals
appropriately, meeting needs I didn't
even know were there.*

God, My Protector

O Lord my God, I take refuge in you; save and deliver me from all who pursue me.

O Lord my God, I take refuge in you; save and deliver me from all who pursue me,
or they will tear me like a lion and rip me to pieces with no one to rescue me.
O Lord my God, if I have done this and there is guilt on my hands —
if I have done evil to him who is at peace with me or without cause have robbed my foe —
then let my enemy pursue and overtake me; let him trample my life to the ground and make me sleep in the dust. — Selah
Arise, O Lord, in your anger; rise up against the rage of my enemies. Awake, my God; decree justice.
Let the assembled peoples gather around you. Rule over them from on high;
let the Lord judge the peoples. Judge me, O Lord, according to my righteousness, according to my integrity, O Most High.
O righteous God, who searches minds and hearts, bring to an end the violence of the wicked and make the righteous secure.

Lord, I am willing to face your judgement. Your discernment is razer-sharp and could destroy me. But it can divide the subtleties of my character as well. It can sharpen the truth while piercing the root of wickedness. I am willing to take the risk of your justice, Lord.

Consequences of Evil

I will give thanks to the Lord because of his righteousness.

My shield is God Most High, who saves the upright in heart.
God is a righteous judge, a God who expresses his wrath every day.
If he does not relent, he will sharpen his sword; he will bend and string his bow.
He has prepared his deadly weapons; he makes ready his flaming arrows.
He who is pregnant with evil and conceives trouble gives birth to disillusionment.
He who digs a hole and scoops it out falls into the pit he has made.
The trouble he causes recoils on himself; his violence comes down on his own head.
I will give thanks to the Lord because of his righteousness and will sing praise to the name of the Lord Most High.

You who are King of heaven and earth, will bring the violence of the wicked upon themselves. We who are impatient for you to do this do not realize you are waiting on our behalf, waiting until we mature. You cannot destroy the thistles without damaging the grain. We want to be ready for harvest. Teach us to trust your timing.

Children's Song

How majestic is your name in all the earth!

O Lord, our.Lord, how majestic is your name in all the earth!
You have set your glory above the heavens.
From the lips of children and infants you have ordained praise because of your enemies, to silence the foe and the avenger.
When I consider your heavens, the work of your fingers, the moon and the stars, which you have set in place,
what is man that you are mindful of him, the son of man that you care for him?
You made him a little lower than the heavenly beings and crowned him with glory and honor.
You made him ruler over the works of your hands; you put everything under his feet:
all flocks and herds, and the beasts of the field,
the birds of the air, and the fish of the sea, all that swim the paths of the seas.
O Lord, our Lord, how majestic is your name in all the earth!

There should always be a two-year old in the house! No one else can keep us so intimately in touch with what we really are: the most sacred yet elemental stuff of creation. Nor can anyone but a two-year-old keep us so aware of the honor with which God has crowned mankind: counting us worthy of redemption, though we are all just two-year-olds at heart.

Tell of Wonderful Things

*The Lord is a refuge for the oppressed, for you,
Lord, have never forsaken those who seek you.*

I will praise you, O Lord, with all my heart; I will tell of
all your wonders.
I will be glad and rejoice in you; I will sing praise to your
name, O Most High.
My enemies turn back; they stumble and perish before
you.
For you have upheld my right and my cause; you have
sat on your throne, judging righteously.
You have rebuked the nations and destroyed the
wicked; you have blotted out their name for ever and
ever.
Endless ruin has overtaken the enemy, you have
uprooted their cities; even the memory of them has
perished.
The Lord reigns forever; He has established his throne
for judgment.
He will judge the world in righteousness; he will govern
the peoples with justice.
The Lord is a refuge for the oppressed, a stronghold in
times of trouble.
Those who know your name will trust in you, for you,
Lord, have never forsaken those who seek you.

*Dandelion seeds driven by the breeze
are an amusing sight, each one a
life-bringer. I stand alone at times
feeling oppressed and quite useless.
But you breathe your Spirit upon me,
and count the possibilities in what I
figured was finished.*

God Does Not Forget

He does not ignore the cry of the afflicted.

Sing praises to the Lord, enthroned in Zion; proclaim among the nations what he has done.
For he who avenges blood remembers; he does not ignore the cry of the afflicted.

O Lord, see how my enemies persecute me! Have mercy and lift me up from the gates of death,
that I may declare your praises in the gates of the Daughter of Zion and there rejoice in your salvation.
The nations have fallen into the pit they have dug; their feet are caught in the net they have hidden.
The Lord is known by his justice; the wicked are ensnared by the work of their hands. — Selah

The wicked return to the grave, all the nations that forget God.
But the needy will not always be forgotten, nor the hope of the afflicted ever perish.

Arise, O Lord, let not man triumph; let the nations be judged in your presence.
Strike them with terror, O Lord; let the nations know they are but men. — Selah

Lord, you listen compassionately to the cries echoing around the world, cries that make our hearts ache. You hear other cries which we are deaf to, though they often come from our own backyard. You hear our helpless comments, witness our frail attempts to reach out. How can we help to undo what we have stood by and watched in silence? You are the Lord of the needy. Do not let our indifference prevail.

In Times of Trouble

Why, O Lord, do you stand far off? Why do you hide yourself in times of trouble?

Why, O Lord, do you stand far off? Why do you hide yourself in times of trouble?

In his arrogance the wicked man hunts down the weak, who are caught in the schemes he devises.

He boasts of the cravings of his heart; he blesses the greedy and reviles the Lord.

In his pride the wicked does not seek him; in all his thoughts there is no room for God.

His ways are always prosperous; he is haughty and your laws are far from him; he sneers at all his enemies.

He says to himself, "Nothing will shake me; I'll always be happy and never have trouble."

His mouth is full of curses and lies and threats; trouble and evil are under his tongue.

He lies in wait near the villages; from ambush he murders the innocent, watching in secret for his victims.

He lies in wait like a lion in cover; he lies in wait to catch the helpless; he catches the helpless and drags them off in his net.

His victims are crushed, they collapse; they fall under his strength.

He says to himself, "God has forgotten; he covers his face and never sees."

There are times when your back is turned to your children. You challenge us to answer our own questions. The world feeds on its own violence and you allow us to face it alone. We are not ploys of fate, neither is our destiny in our own hands. There are times when you turn your back, but you are still in control.

When I consider Your heavens,
the work of Your fingers,
The moon and the stars,
which You have ordained,
What is man that You are
mindful of him,
And the son of man that
You visit him?

Those with Needs

O Lord, you encourage them, and you listen to their cry, defending the fatherless and the oppressed.

Arise, Lord! Lift up your hand, O God. Do not forget the helpless.
Why does the wicked man revile God? Why does he say to himself, "He won't call me to account"?
But you, O God, do see trouble and grief; you consider it to take it in hand. The victim commits himself to you; you are the helper of the fatherless.
Break the arm of the wicked and evil man; call him to account for his wickedness that would not be found out.

The Lord is King for ever and ever; the nations will perish from his land.
You hear, O Lord, the desire of the afflicted; you encourage them, and you listen to their cry, defending the fatherless and the oppressed, in order that man, who is of the earth, may terrify no more.

Prepare my heart, Father. Prepare it to receive with grace what you are about to give. Prepare it to receive new desires, the desires of your heart. Prepare it for worship and fellowship with you.

Safety

In the Lord I take refuge.

**In the Lord I take refuge. How then can you say to me:
"Flee like a bird to your mountain.
For look, the wicked bend their bows; they set their
arrows against the strings to shoot from the shadows at
the upright in heart.
When the foundations are being destroyed, what can the
righteous do?"
The Lord is in his holy temple; the Lord is on his
heavenly throne. He observes the sons of men; his eyes
examine them.
The Lord examines the righteous, but the wicked and
those who love violence his soul hates.
On the wicked he will rain fiery coals and burning sulfur;
a scorching wind will be their lot.
For the Lord is righteous, he loves justice; upright men
will see his face.**

*There are people a-plenty who are
content to live for themselves, who
fail to see further than the borders of
their own existence. I feel the
temptation to give up caring as well,
confronting the fact of my
inadequacy. But I put my trust in
you, Lord, and believe you will test my
willingness to be used. Only then can
your compassion reach others through
me.*

The Promises of God

"Because of the oppression of the weak and the groaning of the needy, I will now arise," says the Lord. "I will protect them from those who malign them."

Help, Lord, for the godly are no more; the faithful have vanished from among men.
Everyone lies to his neighbor; their flattering lips speak with deception.
May the Lord cut off all flattering lips and every boastful tongue that says,
"We will triumph with our tongues; we own our lips — who is our master?"
"Because of the oppression of the weak and the groaning of the needy, I will now arise," says the Lord. "I will protect them from those who malign them."
And the words of the Lord are flawless, like silver refined in a furnace of clay, purified seven times.
O Lord, you will keep us safe and protect us from such people forever.
The wicked freely strut about when what is vile is honored among men.

Values are twisted. Self has become the basis of ethic; feelings, the plumb-line for morality. Virtue and purity have long since fallen into disrepute. The sighs of the humble are riden by the taunts of the proud. Yet, there is something to be said for the fact that the sighs remain at all. They are the salt and intercession without which the world could not survive.

When God Hides Himself

But I trust in your unfailing love.

How long, O Lord? Will you forget me forever? How long will you hide your face from me?
How long must I wrestle with my thoughts and every day have sorrow in my heart? How long will my enemy triumph over me?
Look on me and answer, O Lord my God. Give light to my eyes, or I will sleep in death;
my enemy will say, "I have overcome him," and my foes will rejoice when I fall.
But I trust in your unfailing love; my heart rejoices in your salvation.
I will sing to the Lord, for he has been good to me.

The ability to envision the bounty of summer's harvest in the midst of winter is truely a gift of God. Winter often seems disproportionately long. But waiting seems longest when spring is the closest. I am learning to recognize the seasons of God's dealings and to understand the need for each at its proper time.

Expectations

Oh, that salvation for Israel would come out of Zion!

The fool says in his heart, "There is no God." They are corrupt, their deeds are vile; there is no one who does good.

The Lord looks down from heaven on the sons of men to see if there are any who understand, any who seek God.

All have turned aside, they have together become corrupt; there is no one who does good, not even one.

Will evildoers never learn — those who devour my people as men eat bread and who do not call on the Lord?

There they are, overwhelmed with dread, for God is present in the company of the righteous.

You evildoers frustrate the plans of the poor, but the Lord is their refuge.

Oh, that salvation for Israel would come out of Zion! When the Lord restores the fortunes of his people, let Jacob rejoice and Israel be glad!

Lord, I seem to be wishing for what I can't have. I base my expectations upon the acquisitions of friends and neighbors. How quickly I forget on the descent from the mountain the simplicity of living a godly life. Keep me from turning aside towards trivialities as we walk the way of salvation.

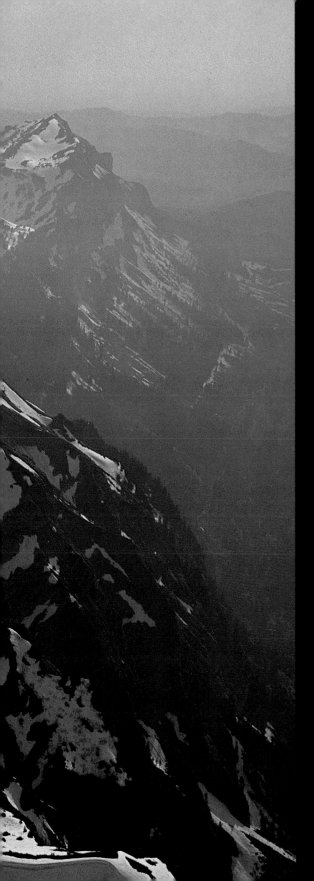

Safe from Enemies

He who does these things will never be shaken.

Lord, who may dwell in your sanctuary? Who may live
on your holy hill?
He whose walk is blameless and who does what is
righteous, who speaks the truth from his heart
and has no slander on his tongue, who does his neighbor
no wrong and casts no slur on his fellow man,
who despises a vile man but honors those who fear the
Lord, who keeps his oath even when it hurts,
who lends his money without usury and does not accept
a bribe against the innocent.
He who does these things will never be shaken.

*My Grandmother frequently
admonished, »Do what's right with all
His might!« As I meditate on your
word, Lord, I realize the might
originates with you, but the choice to
do what is right is up to me. You are
present to help solidify my will at the
crossroads of daily decisions, and to
stabilize my moods when, fluxuating,
they would otherwise determine my
emotions. Granny knew a secret and
I'm glad she loved to share it.*

All I Need

"You are my Lord; apart from you I have no good thing."

Keep me safe, O God, for in you I take refuge.
I said to the Lord, "You are my Lord; apart from you I have no good thing."
As for the saints who are in the land, they are the glorious ones in whom is all my delight.
The sorrows of those will increase who run after other gods. I will not pour out their libations of blood or take up their names on my lips.

Lord, you have assigned me my portion and my cup; you have made my lot secure.
The boundary lines have fallen for me in pleasant places; surely I have a delightful inheritance.
I will praise the Lord, who counsels me; even at night my heart instructs me.

Lord, you counsel me to raise my expectations, to absorb the fellowship of the saints, to believe in the best when I might settle for the good. You gave the Holy Spirit that I might walk in confidence even when the lights go out.

O LORD, our Lord,
How excellent is Your name
in all the earth!

Joy in His Presence

I have set the Lord always before me.

I have set the Lord always before me. Because he is at my right hand, I will not be shaken.

Therefore my heart is glad and my tongue rejoices; my body also will rest secure,
because you will not abandon me to the grave, nor will you let your Holy One see decay.
You have made known to me the path of life; you will fill me with joy in your presence, with eternal pleasures at your right hand.

You have made my spirit dance even when crossing troubled waters. You have taken the dread out of facing the fact that I must one day die. The path ahead is an bright as your promises. All this because I have decided to believe that you are with me. And you reward my trust!

The Lord Lives!

O Lord, give ear to my prayer — it does not rise
from deceitful lips.

Hear, O Lord, my righteous plea; listen to my cry. Give
ear to my prayer — it does not rise from deceitful lips.
May my vindication come from you; may your eyes see
what is right.

Though you probe my heart and examine me at night,
though you test me, you will find nothing; I have
resolved that my mouth will not sin.

As for the deeds of men — by the word of your lips I
have kept myself from the ways of the violent.

My steps have held to your paths; my feet have not
slipped.

You walked ahead of me, Lord, and I
felt lonely on the way. At night you
turned back and found me still
following. You stayed beside me for
a while. At dawn I saw the reason you
must hurry on: to clear the path of
snares.

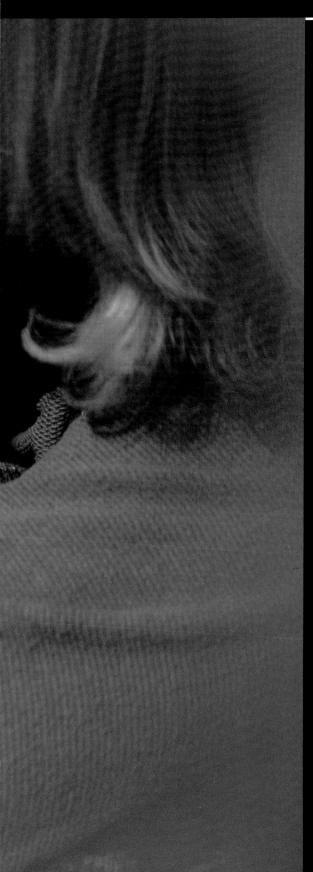

Wonderful Love

O God, give ear to me and hear my prayer.

I call on you, O God, for you will answer me; give ear to me and hear my prayer.
Show the wonder of your great love, you who save by your right hand those who take refuge in you from their foes.
Keep me as the apple of your eye; hide me in the shadow of your wings
from the wicked who assail me, from my mortal enemies who surround me.

They close up their callous hearts, and their mouths speak with arrogance.
They have tracked me down, they now surround me, with eyes alert, to throw me to the ground.
They are like a lion hungry for prey, like a great lion crouching in cover.
Rise up, O Lord, confront them, bring them down; rescue me from the wicked by your sword.
O Lord, by your hand save me from such men, from men of this world whose reward is in this life.

You still the hunger of those you cherish; their sons have plenty, and they store up wealth for their children.
And I — in righteousness I will see your face; when I awake, I will be satisfied with seeing your likeness.

Lord, forbid that I should have my entire portion in this life. Often, those who have the important miss the essential. Sooner or later I will have to make a decision. I can choose to store up treasures on earth or to invest my assets in your kingdom.

Rescue in Trouble

I love you, O Lord, my strength.

The Lord is my rock, my fortress and my deliverer; my God is my rock, in whom I take refuge. He is my shield and the horn of my salvation, my stronghold. I call to the Lord, who is worthy of praise, and I am saved from my enemies.

My expressions of love for you, Lord, are not merely pious mutterings. They are earnest essentials based on past experience and expectations for the future. Like bedtime whisperings between husband and wife, they fill the gaps of relationship occuring during the day, adding mortar and brick to our fortification of devotion.

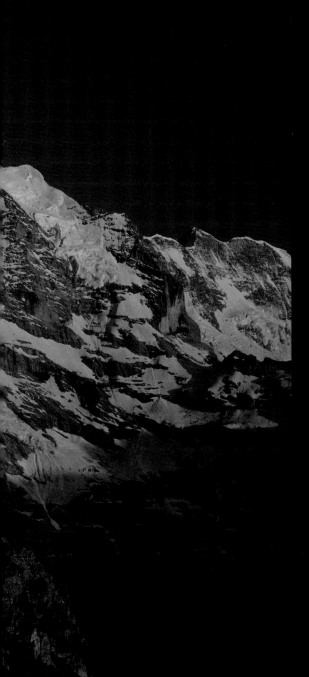

Majesty of God

From his temple he heard my voice.

The cords of death entangled me; the torrents of destruction overwhelmed me.
The cords of the grave coiled around me; the snares of death confronted me.
In my distress I called to the Lord; I cried to my God for help. From his temple he heard my voice; my cry came before him, into his ears.
The earth trembled and quaked, and the foundations of the mountains shook; they trembled because he was angry.
Smoke rose from his nostrils; consuming fire came from his mouth, burning coals blazed out of it.
He parted the heavens and came down; dark clouds were under his feet.
He mounted the cherubim and flew; he soared on the wings of the wind.
He made darkness his covering, his canopy around him — the dark rain clouds of the sky.
Out of the brightness of his presence clouds advanced, with hailstones and bolts of lightning.

God, your magnificence stirs my imagination. How could I ever presume to feel that I know you, for you express yourself in fresh images when I least expect it. You take me by surprize and fill my soul with shimmering wonder.

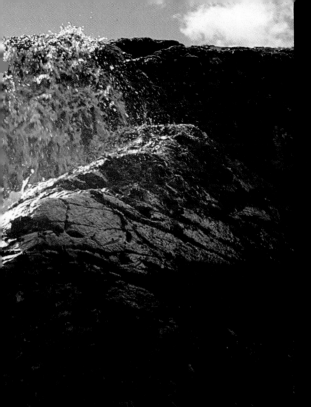

Entering God's Presence

He brought me out into a spacious place. He rescued me.

The Lord thundered from heaven; the voice of the Most High resounded.
He shot his arrows and scattered the enemies, great bolts of lightning and routed them.
The valleys of the sea were exposed and the foundations of the earth laid bare at your rebuke, O Lord, at the blast of breath from your nostrils.
He reached down from on high and took hold of me; he drew me out of deep waters.
He rescued me from my powerful enemy, from my foes, who were too strong for me.
They confronted me in the day of my disaster, but the Lord was my support.
He brought me out into a spacious place; he rescued me because he delighted in me.

Unrelenting pressures nearly carried me away with them. I was ready to sink rather than to fight back or even to hang on. Lord, you reached into the tumultuous waters. Your everlasting arms supported me. You didn't let the maelstrom take control.

Light in Darkness

With my God I can scale a wall.

The Lord has dealt with me according to my righteousness; according to the cleanness of my hands he has rewarded me.
For I have kept the ways of the Lord; I have not done evil by turning from my God.
All his laws are before me; I have not turned away from his decrees.
I have been blameless before him and have kept myself from sin.
The Lord has rewarded me according to my righteousness, according to the cleanness of my hands in his sight.

To the faithful you show yourself faithful, to the pure you show yourself pure, but to the crooked you show yourself shrewd.
You save the humble but bring low those whose eyes are haughty.
You, O Lord, keep my lamp burning; my God turns my darkness into light.
With your help I can advance against a troop; with my God I can scale a wall.

As for God, his way is perfect; the word of the Lord is flawless. He is a shield for all who take refuge in him.

Ambition and aggression are rewarded by shrewd accomplishment. They are virtues in the realm of this world. Mercy, humility, purity are keys to a different kingdom. I will keep my gaze steady in your direction, Lord. Whatever success I achieve, may it be by your light.

I have set the LORD always before me;
Because He is at my right hand
I shall not be moved.

Foothold on the Mountains

Who is the Rock except our God?

For who is God besides the Lord? And who is the Rock except our God?

It is God who arms me with strength and makes my way perfect.

He makes my feet like the feet of a deer; he enables me to stand on the heights.

He trains my hands for battle; my arms can bend a bow of bronze.

You give me your shield of victory, and your right hand sustains me; you stoop down to make me great.

You broaden the path beneath me, so that my ankles do not turn.

I pursued my enemies and overtook them; I did not turn back till they were destroyed.

I crushed them so that they could not rise; they fell beneath my feet.

You armed me with strength for battle; you made my adversaries bow at my feet.

You made my enemies turn their back in flight, and I destroyed my foes.

They cried for help, but there was no one to save them — to the Lord, but he did not answer.

I beat them as fine as dust borne on the wind; I poured them out like mud in the streets.

Perfection is a high standard. But who or what is it that can set me in places I've never dared reach out towards before? It is you, Lord. I relied on your tenderness and it gave me strength. I relied on your wisdom and it made me successful. My future belongs to you. I may never be perfect, but I can be a vessel for your glory.

God's Way

You exalted me above my foes.

You have delivered me from the attacks of the people; you have made me the head of nations; people I did not know are subject to me.
As soon as they hear me, they obey me; foreigners cringe before me.
They all lose heart; they come trembling from their strongholds.
The Lord lives! Praise be to my Rock! Exalted be God my Savior!
He is the God who avenges me, who subdues nations under me,
who saves me from my enemies. You exalted me above my foes; from violent men you rescued me.
Therefore I will praise you among the nations, O Lord; I will sing praises to your name.
He gives his king great victories; he shows unfailing kindness to his anointed, to David and his descendants forever.

You have brought me close to you, Lord, so close I can nearly look up into your face. You have brought me to new heights of knowing you. Yet, this is only the beginning. How much higher can I get? The highest place of all is there where I kneel at the foot of the cross.

God's Glory in Creation

*Day after day they pour forth speech; night after
night they display knowledge.*

The heavens declare the glory of God; the skies
proclaim the work of his hands.
Day after day they pour forth speech; night after night
they display knowledge.
There is no speech or language where their voice is not
heard.
Their voice goes out into all the earth, their words to the
ends of the world.
In the heavens he has pitched a tent for the sun,
which is like a bridegroom coming forth from his
pavilion, like a champion rejoicing to run his course.
It rises at one end of the heavens and makes its circuit to
the other; nothing is hidden from its heat.

*In each corner of the earth, creation
wears a different garment, yet
proclaims the same message. Hidden
in the expressions of God's majesty
are promises of redemption. If we
interpret these correctly, we will
recognize the Bridegroom-Messiah
and anticipate his return.*

I will praise You, O LORD,
with my whole heart;
I will tell of all
Your marvelous works.

The Lord is my
rock and my fortress and
my deliverer; My God, my strength,
in whom I will trust; My shield and the horn
of my salvation, my stronghold. I will call upon the Lord,
who is worthy to be praised; So shall I be saved
from my enemies. The pangs of death
encompassed me, And the floods of
ungodliness made me afraid.